# Sky Holding Fall

## Poems
## by
## Judy Bebelaar

BLUE LIGHT PRESS ◆ 1ST WORLD PUBLISHING

SAN FRANCISCO ◆ FAIRFIELD ◆ DELHI

1st WORLD LIBRARY
PO Box 2211
Fairfield, IA 52556
www.1stworldpublishing.com

BLUE LIGHT PRESS
www.bluelightpress.com
bluelightpress@aol.com

BOOK & COVER DESIGN
Melanie Gendron
gentarot@comcast.net

COVER PHOTO
Alan Jencks

AUTHOR PHOTO
Laurie Bell Bishop
laurie@laurieb.photography

FIRST EDITION

Library of Congress Cataloging-in-Publication Data

ISBN: 978-1-4218-3546-4

# Praise for Sky Holding Fall

*Sky Holding Fall*, Judy Bebelaar's long-awaited collection, holds all the great subjects – life and death, love and loss, light and dark. But always, even as she acknowledges the darkest moments – her mother's depression, her young husband's death to cancer, her own cancer, the world's difficult truths – Bebelaar returns us to light. Through keenly observed images and a richness of particulars – surf boards, pill bottles filled with buttons, a woman's prayer stone, a hand-hewn cedar bed – Bebelaar makes us see what it means to live life fully in all its "sad lovely tumult." Her poems comfort and console even as they challenge us to live our own lives just as fully and fearlessly as we find life's "small miracles," which Bebelaar offers us over and over again in these beautifully accomplished poems.

> – Lynne Knight, author of *The Language of Forgetting*

In Judy Bebelaar's poem, "Bitter Tea," she says, "pain becomes a teacher." The Chinese have a saying, "Eat bitter," that is, learn to endure the pain, and this powerful new collection has plenty of that: a chronically depressed mother, a beloved husband who dies too young, the assault of breast cancer. When Judy says, "how can any of us/say the ways/we are changed," she means changed by irrefutable mortality and its ravages. And yet *Sky Holding Fall* is one long lyrical saying – let's call it testimony – to how we survive those changes: through cherishable memory, through the felicities of simple pleasures, and most of all through the love of everything that is still here to be loved. As well as this welcome reminder: "…sometimes," she says, "it is possible/to make our own miracles."

> – Thomas Centolella, author of *Almost Human*

*Sky Holding Fall* explores grief and its passage with a voice that is both brave and expansive. These poems surmount the paradox of "what cannot be said, /but must be said," not only with unflinching scrutiny, but more importantly, with lyrical deftness and a painterly eye, moving effortlessly between the narrative and the metaphorical. Judy Bebelaar confronts both personal pain and the joy of life a with a poetic eye and cosmic grace.

> – Jeanne Wagner, author of *Everything Turns Into Something Else*

How do we perceive death with its lingering light spreading memories like morning dew quickly drying in the brightening sun? How do we maintain a balance between the personal, private I, and the public shared we? There is a way that poetry, that poems can be both personal and universal, can be dressed in elegant language while revealing naked pain, courage and integrity. *Sky Holding Fall* does all of this. Judy Bebelaar has written a book of seeing and connection, of everyday miracles and astronomy, of birdsong and sea, and forests holding mountains, all reaching toward a changing sky. It is a book of the human capacity to face death, to revel in life, and to love and love again.

> – devorah major, San Francisco's Third Poet Laureate,
> author of *Califia's Daughters*

This book is dedicated to
California Poets in the Schools
and to all the poets who visited my classes
during my 37 years
as a San Francisco high school teacher.

Among the many:

Francisco X Alarcon

Duane BigEagle

Wifredo Castaño

Thomas Centolella

Victor Hernandez Cruz

Ruth Gendler

Jessica Haggedorn

Katharine Harer

Juan Felipe Herrera

Uchechi Kalu

Genny Lim

devorah major

Gail Newman

Simon Ortiz

Floyd Salas

Mona Lisa Saloy

Sonia Sanchez

Al Young

# Table of Contents

## Part III    Sky Holding Fall

## Part IV    Boat Full of Sky

# Part I
## Something

# Something

This has something to do with the *tap tap tap* of an early morning dream,
with traffic rushing by and people who talk too much,
with jet exhaust and red-tailed hawks.
This has something to do with plum blossoms every February.
And then hard rain.

Something to do with the curve of future plans,
with Esalen, Constantinople, Positano, and the French Riviera,
with trips that may never be made and hope gone awry,
with fires, full lunar eclipses,
and sudden gusts of wind
blowing down fifty-year-old elms,
with nests falling out of trees.

This has something to do with swimming
all the way to the raft,
and lying on hot wood with silty water drying on your skin,
a hand flung over your eyes to keep out the sun.

Something to do with wars and babies,
with uterine cancer
and a nice calm game of draw poker.
Something to do with birthdays,
and friends, and just-missed trains.

With cedar and spring bamboo,
with shades of green and yellow in a sun-struck cornfield,
with the gaze directed at the horizon,
and balance, with moss
between stones, with blue between patches of clouds,
and the moment between inhale and exhale.

Something to do with how he died that beautiful June,
and with how improbable it was that I met you
because of a broken hinge on a broken door,
now the door to our bedroom
made lovely by your hands.

# Bitter Tea

When your husband, 42, is diagnosed
with an untreatable lymphoma,
which may kill him within a year,
or twenty years —

and you're brewing a bitter tea you buy in Chinatown,
pulled from beautiful drawers on the wall:
bits of dried things that look like roots,
shriveled dark leaves, bits of woody stuff
that must be boiled for hours,
watchfully, so it doesn't burn,
which it often does,
and burnt or not,
a pungent smell of old dead things
permeates the house.

When you're trying for a miracle,
trying to live by the anti-cancer mantra
prescribed by his surf mate:
*More surf, more sex; less work, less stress,*
pain becomes a teacher.

You find it confusing that John was feeling strong, healthy —
except for lumps that grew,
and then shrank —
usually.
Going to work, he always knotted his tie
to hide the collar button,
undone for the most stubborn tumor
at his throat.

You begin to learn
to slide out from under
the hopelessness that can drape itself over you
anywhere: when you buy
macrobiotic brown rice
and shiitake mushrooms at Yasai
or you have to pull over
when driving alone up a leafy hill above the sea
to a teacher meeting at the Headlands.

In your classroom, afternoon light
slants through the window –
how he loved sunlight through leaves –
and the pigeons in the courtyard,
empty now of raucous teenagers,
make their own happy racket.
Seventeen-year-old Patty says, *Ms. B?*
*Can I read you the poem I wrote*
*that time your husband called you*
*from the hospital – remember, I was there?*
I smile: *Please.*

*I saw the glass,*
*bright tubing that formed your veins;*
*I saw you smile on the phone*
*and I knew it was him.*

Sometimes it seems,
remembering a moment,
that you are there.
In the hospital you
whispered loud in his ear,
as he lay dying,
friends gathered bedside,
*Does it feel good, Babe,*
*when we touch you?*

And after not moving,
not speaking
for many hours,
he slowly,
with great deliberation,
lifted his head from the pillow
and nodded

*yes.*

## Ode to Broken Things

When things break
it's no one's fault, according to Neruda.

It used to be we mended things –
darned socks and hammered out bent forks.
But now we throw out cracked pottery,
frames with smashed glass,
sofas sagging from squashed coils;
de-silvered mirrors and three-legged chairs
we leave curbside for ragged men with grocery carts.

But Grandma Oberg's chipped Haviland platter,
gold rim faded, rests safely hidden
far back on the top shelf
of the lead glass cupboard.
And always there is a jar of stashed pens
which will never write again,
or a child's rocker languishing in the garage
waiting for glue and clamps

and in the backs of drawers, jewelry
with broken clasps and chains,
old watches that won't work,
something in the intricate system of gears gone wrong.

I confess I am part of the conspiracy
to save these broken things.
Some sentimental streak,
some softness in me that perhaps
should have hardened by now.

Come to me, spirit of Neruda,
you with your transcendental glue of odes
welding oceans and eyes, watermelons and trees,
kisses and poppies, love and dead doves.

Help me mend everything, make what's broken whole,
sew up the doll ripped in two,
place children breathing again
back into arms of grieving mothers,
sling up the fallen stars in fiery arcs,
place hand in hand all the lovers
torn apart by accident or fatal illness,
stupidity of war,
restore the plundered forests with fragrant sap.

# Persimmon

In the snapshot he balances it
on his bald head.
The smile under that glowing fruit
is complicated.

I can see him, before he got sick,
his hair tamed into a ponytail by a rubber band.
I laughed when he told me
that one of his students, a girl
in his English class at Richmond High,
asked if she could touch his hair:
*Why Mr. B, your hair is nappy like mine!*

After the chemo all John's thick curly brown hair
fell out in clumps in the shower
over a few days.

I bought, as a present for him,
a persimmon tree.
He loved to see the orange fruit
on bare winter limbs.
I love that last year
the tree, transplanted three times,
bore the most fruit it ever has.
Soon it will be older
than he was
when he died.

Soon the leaves will burnish
then fall, in a few days,
as they always do,
in a bright heap.

# Names

*inspired by Pablo Neruda's "Too Many Names"*

What is the name of the dream
that will not be called up,
but teases you with loose bits:
a swimming pool, a narrow bed,
a ladder in the rain?

When I spoke to a mountain
it answered me with a stone
in a stream, told me neither
the name of the stone – or its own.

Burma becomes Myanmar,
Tibet, China and there is blood
in the streets, monks imprisoned,
torture. If countries had no names
would we have no wars?

We say *my name is* or *I am called*
 or *je m'apelle* – I call myself –
as if we know our names are not ourselves,
just something borrowed, a worn cloak,
a covering that does not cover.

Neruda wants to *confuse* things, he says,
to *undress* them so that there is only wholeness,
the crisp smell of life:
ocean, island, flower, bee, child, bear: all one.
He says there are too many names.
And yet they are all we have.

# Gliding

They are thigh to thigh in the narrow seat,
dipping, turning
on insubstantial air.
The pilot wonders if they'd like to do a loop.
He wants to answer yes, but he asks her first.
She's afraid, so he tells the pilot no.

They are in love. Or she is in love.
It's too soon.
He's too young.
She is in love with his arm
around her shoulders.
It's been so long.

Or in love with the curly crowd of blond hairs
glistening on his brown forearm,
muscled from hammer and saw,
with the smile in his voice on the phone.
But up here, floating
with the raptors, who can tell?

They don't talk, sitting so close,
looking down at vineyards,
barns, canopied oaks
spread out like illustrations in a children's book.
The glider rattles.
But she doesn't hear.

She's thinking she wouldn't mind
if he kissed her.
But it's too soon
after her husband's death.

He was too young to die,
and she's old enough to know better.
Isn't she?
She's probably just
a little giddy
up here,
so far above the earth.

# Esalen

All I can hear is the sure, steady sound
of waves shouldering in.
So it's almost possible to believe,
if I see that misty white signal,
that the whales are still traveling the old sea roads.

Just now I can't bear to think of starfish,
deformed, or dying dolphins,
or my sister who's in a rehab called
Lifecare of Charleston,
who says she's fine,
I shouldn't worry.

All I ask is to look at this wide sea.
Just now it is shining
and a whale – a whole pod of them –
could be out there
heading for the Sea of Cortez.

## Some Birds

We are locked in
to our pasts.
We are books
written by authors
whose names we have forgotten,
living as in a dream
until something pushes us
over the edge
and we wake up,
feel the chill at the sky's corners.
*Already*, we notice.
*So soon this year*, we think,
the leaves turning,
the squirrels beginning to nibble
at the green persimmons,
and finding them bitter,
throw them down.
Still, some birds sing.
The finches have fledged,
moved on,
so small and trim,
so focused on being alive.

# Swimming in the Cochlea

*Full fathom five thy father lies;*
*Of his bones are coral made;*
*Those are pearls that were his eyes:*
*Nothing of him that doth fade,*
*But doth suffer a sea-change. – The Tempest*

Three glistening curves
Silver, pink, the colors of
The hushed roar of sea sounds
Mother of pearl, abalone shell

Sea changes
*Those were pearls*
His eyes were blue
The dark pupil floating
In the iris ocean

The blood, they say, is an ancient sea,
Watery, the salt, the other ions
So like the sea's

And the cochlea of the inner ear,
A chambered nautilus,
A golden section of sea flesh

When a memory flashes
The little Mexican restaurant
On the way to Asilomar
And the room with yellow wallpaper
That smile when he came out of the water
Little River, below Big Sur

Then he's not gone
And now means nothing
Gone as quickly as it's said

Is that the shadow of a cloud on the sea,
Or a forest of kelp?

*Those were pearls*
His eyes
Sea changes

## April: Irene

In London, on the way to the Royal Shakespeare,
she didn't want me to take her picture
in the back of the cab.
I wish I had.

She was wearing the red scarf I gave her.
She looked beautiful and happy,
sitting next to John.

Today she says *If it weren't for being sick,*
*I'd like this time of my life,*
*things moving so slowly.*
*And the book is almost finished.*
We look at some of the pages.
*It will be simpler than this,*
*more space on the page,*
*a picture between each section.*

Now we go to the kitchen,
share a fig, miso soup.
She tells me about Hawaii.
*I couldn't go out much, too sick.*
*But these wonderful small birds,*
*finches, we think,*
*built their nest of coconut fibers*
*right on the bedroom windowsill,*
*just outside the screen.*
*It even had a roof,*
*and by the day we had to leave,*
*there were five tiny eggs.*

We go to the computer;
she finds the birds for me.

The nest is a brown bower,
ragged and sweet.
Then she is tired.
We go back to her bedroom.
I open the window to blue sky, tree, breeze.
She doesn't say she's in pain.
*I keep it way up here on the dresser*
*so the dog won't find it.*
The lollypop is methadone.

She climbs back into bed.
I say, *I'm going to buy bulbs*
*at the nursery. Shall I buy you some too?*
Then I bite my tongue.
Certain words
must be approached with care:
*next spring*, or *in the summer*.
I count six months.
That's what she said on the phone.
*Six months*. April.

Not tulips, they would bloom in May, maybe June.
Daffodils, or hyacinth?
*I'll get both of us paper white narcissus.*
I say.
*You can put them in a bowl indoors.*
*They'll think it's spring.*

Her eyes are open.
So are mine.
But there is a terrible looseness,
a slack in the soul, the unraveling
of time. In my mind's eye,
the birds in their bower nest,
the five tiny eggs.

She sees them too.

# Red-Tailed Hawk

In spring's green ease
a pair of red-tailed hawks
draws slow circles
high above a windy field.

The male begins to plummet
and rise, over and over,
a miracle of arc and reach,
his eyes, cut obsidian, yellow fire.
He touches her, and then the two,
pulling light through wide-spread feathers,
grasp talons and spiral down,
a wild courtship
against brilliant coastal blue.

From the shambles of summer
they weave a nest
from wildness,
wind in grass,
steady beat of sea on rock,
bark and husks and stalks.

Autumn, her chicks soft and wary,
watch from a tall eucalyptus
as the female circles over the field,
hovers, then slips down,
a flash of darkness trailing light.
Her mate, nearby
follows her sweep
to the grass.

# Surfboards

My husband's desk, with piles of papers in rubber bands,
was dwarfed by the circle of *sticks*:
that's what surfers call them –
graceful ellipses, six feet or so, coated on top with layers of wax,
gritty and gray with sand from beaches like Año,
Pacifica, Ocean Beach, Salmon Creek,
the river mouth at Jenner.

    He'd slide into me kneeling and grinning,
    one browned arm out like a wing,
    the other hand guiding the board
    on its way down the wave face that glinted in the sun.

On the nose of the board
two dolphins forming a yin-yang,
his sea brothers, his guardian spirits.
We didn't know the legends:
all the dolphins who rescued drowning humans,

    didn't know his dolphins wouldn't save him
    from the cancer swimming in his lymphatic system
    but when he surfed they were with him
    and surfing, he said, was his religion.

After he died, I gave the first of John's boards away,
the clear one, white with brown stringer and rails,
to Will the plumber.
He'd seen the boards in the crawl space
when he worked on the furnace.
Will said he'd like one to hang in his barn in Omaha.
At first it seemed a good idea
but as he walked down the driveway
the board under his arm
I wondered why I'd ever let it go.

I gave the tan one with dolphins on the deck,
to our daughter, Kristy,
and another like it,
but sky blue, to Pete, John's English knee-boarding mate.
That was right, I knew.
I gave John's old-style longboard to Jason,
now gone, young, like John, and from cancer too,
the two of them riding waves
only in snapshots.

Some of the pictures still surprise me
when I look through the basket:

    there, sliding in at Lighthouse, a five or six-foot wave,
    and on a little one at Sunset Beach,
    turquoise water, soft pink clouds,
    as if nothing could ever go wrong.

Last year I gave Leo the blue and black board,
a college graduation present.
He wrote to me he was fixing the dings,
so he could take it out at Pleasure Point,
bring it to Bali;
and I kept giving the boards away,
the last one at a yard sale to a father and his eager teenage son,
until they were all scattered,
as John's ashes were, at Año,
sifting now through all the oceans of the world.

# Gathering Light

*Guggenheim Museum September 7, 2014 James Turrell Aten Reign*

Light falling
from 18 billion years ago
from stars
or from stage lights
light cascading down like rain,
like a blessing.

My heart beats more slowly as the soft blue
deepens shade by shade
into royal blue at the lowest tier
of the rotunda's ascending spheres
and already the light falling
from the highest sphere in the dome
is now rose,

becoming warmer as it spills
from each ring of light
and my breath quickens,
my heart pumps time away
faster
and yet here we are
in a timeless realm

of falling light
mesmerized by yellow now
into peach and the world outside
with its racket and clatter,
its cursing and spitting
less real than the light falling all around
like the light near water,
we silent watchers bound
to one another by the falling light.

21

# Part II
## The Blue and the Dark

## She Sewed

Mother carried the Wheeler-Wilson over the Rockies
to Long Beach in 1929 in the back of their Model T.
She wore riding boots and jodhpurs, dazzled my father's camera
with her blonde bob, her smile.

Four drawers with wreaths around the knobs
hold wooden spools of thread, Belding-Corticelli,
Coats and Clark *bell-waxed, fast to boiling, 15¢*.

When she felt good, she sewed.
She loved robin's egg blue, indigo. Her eyes were China blue.
This spool, the forest green of the six taffeta bridesmaids' dresses
she sewed for Sister's wedding.

She sat and sewed the yarn-haired Raggedy Ann's and Andy's,
Sister's and mine and all the grandchildren's too.
The needle shot through her finger.
The scream pulled me up the stairs from outside.

In this drawer pill bottles full of buttons:
shanked buttons, carved ones, metal buttons to cover with cloth,
buttons from old coats and blouses, all marked and sorted by color:

wooden and jewel-like, round and oval,
and five anchors, all black.
Maybe black because she'd once told me
that at a party a man once told her
*Nothing looks better than a blonde in a black dress and pearls.*
Beautiful, with her hair upswept,
off to the Ritz Poodle Dog in The City where Daddy always wore a hat,
a handkerchief she'd ironed in his suit jacket pocket.

But Swedish girls are taught not to be too proud
and she made it sound like practical advice:
*a blonde in a black dress and pearls.*

Those pill bottles of buttons:
some clearly for her back pain,
Brass buttons, silver buttons, snaps and frogs,
hooks and eyes, but not one of the bottles
that held her pills for depression.

Some days the door to her bedroom
stayed shut all day and the next and the next,
the curtains drawn, the Wheeler-Wilson folded into itself too,
and slanting through the landing window, muffled afternoon sun.

# The Worst

*after Maggie Smith's "What I Carried"*

I wrapped my fear of the worst in a pink flowered blanket
and pushed it around in my doll buggy.
I showed it the camellias and the cactus,
the feathery Pampas grass. The sky.

I carried my fear of the worst that could happen
swaddled in nightmares – the darkened house,
the scared scary face staring out the high window –
my mother's.

I tried to appease my fear of the worst
with heart-shaped buttons we girls wore around our necks,
with notebooks where we wrote our good deeds for the day,
with whitewash on the walls of our shack of a clubhouse.

I worked hard to prevent my fear of the worst
with straight A's and strings of Campfire beads,
with joining up and signing up and meeting up,
always showing up.

I carried my fear of the worst down
to the darkness below the slippery stairs,
strapped it down, chained it up,
locked the door.

But the worst would not shut up or give up. Always,
the worst sneaks out, shows up in a different costume
wears a new mask.

# The Blue and the Dark
*91.7 FM 4:15 pm 9/20/2011*

He was trying to say –
the man who was caught
in the turbine building
that day at Fukushima –
trying to say
what it sounded like:
*demonic*
*and I don't know*
*if it was coming from the earth*
*or the building, the machines,*
*and I thought I would perish*
*there and I prayed aloud*
*for all of us and silently*
*for myself – make it quick*
and he could not say
why he cried, maybe
because he was on high ground
and so many others were
not and he knew
a tsunami was inevitable
and he could not tell
time anymore, how it passed
and after that day he could not sleep
or get on a plane to visit his family
and he has not laughed
or even smiled much since then
how can any of us
say the ways
we are changed –
by the death of a loved one, say,
or after those towers
that will fall

forever, the smoke against
the sky which is still
blue
which is part
of what cannot be said,
but must be said
because somehow
we have to try
to say the blue and the dark
in spite of.

# Sunday

After her father brought her here to play with the twins,
she sat alone in their room on the bottom bunk bed.
She floated in the no-place,
drifting back to before God,
before trees and chickens and eggs,
before Mother, who had gone thin and gray again,
shut in her room again.

Maybe Mother was nowhere too.
Maybe that was what craziness was.
*The sins of the fathers,* Mother would say from her room,
over and over. Then she'd be quiet.
Things almost went white,
and it came, in the hot, dust-glittered air,
the strange-smelling air of a house not your own,
the blank dizzy feeling of maybe not being.

Then Katy and Louise were yelling outside,
and she went out into the stickery summer yard,
the world of hot sidewalks, colored chalk and hopscotch charms
and it was good, even good to help the twins
put salt on snails and watch them curl and sizzle.
It was good to go to the store with Popsicle missiles
and Joe Bazooka bubble gum.

But when that morning came,
the car running in the garage
and Mother fallen down next to the exhaust pipe,
blood blooming by her head,
the void pooled inside
and guilt blossomed too,
like a white silent secret,
and spread to everything.

# What Is That Color of Blue?

*Sydney Walton Park, San Francisco*

This is the quiet center.
A woman whistles softly for a lost dog.
Georgia O'Keefe, bronze, sits solemn on a tree stump
between her solemn huskies.
A two-year-old rides the back of one.
Feathers rustling, a pigeon glides by.
A homeless man, in hardhat and scarf,
pulls his laundry cart of raggedy possessions
to a spot by the fountain, dry now.

Why is the sky so blue in San Francisco?
A sincere blue, a blue that speaks of great hopes,
great loss. Here in this city of a million schemes,
of dashed dreams, this city of Saint Francis
of children and small animals.
*Lord, make me an instrument of thy peace,* he said.
Peace, as elusive as the name of the blue
of the light-filled sky.

So many stories the women could tell.
Those hoping to be sent for when the money was good.
Those brought against their will to work in brothels,
Those hoping for a rich man, maybe a kind man.

Think of the men on sailing ships
lured by the pictures of easy women on shore,
free liquor, laudanum-laced,
shanghaied back to months at sea.

How many Chinese came to Gold Mountain
for work and wealth, and

found instead loneliness, or death.
How many tunnels carved into granite,
how many giant trees felled,
how many men lowered by basket
to ignite a stick of dynamite.

How many Indians died at Mission Dolores,
mission of sorrows? And all the rest?
Count the gravestones,
and multiply by the bell towers
along the Camino Real.

Sit with me, under this willow tree.
Can you name that color of blue?

# Siena

*for Kristy*

I want to return to that place –
the small hotel above Siena's narrow cobbled streets
where hillside angled down to farmland,
midnight mass in the duomo,
lighting candles for your father,
so seemingly indestructible,
gone then six months,
the six foot four of him
now ashes swirling in the seas.

I'm thinking of the soul,
the way it sometimes swells, robust and glowing,
and sometimes curls and shrivels
like fire-blackened paper.

I'm thinking how all that I love in the world –
music, dancing,
plum blossoms against my nose,
the dark etched around my cat's amber eyes,
freshly washed sheets on a new-made bed,
even you,
my only child –

might all have been lost to me,
along with all the tomorrows I have counted on,
if I had not happened upon –
my hand flung over my breast
as I read *The Wings of the Dove* in bed –
the tiny lump
which, impersonal and malevolent
had decided to begin to grow.

I'm thinking how glad I am
that you decided we should go
to that place of green and gold,
of candles flickering in old cathedrals
and carved wooden cherubs.
I'm thinking about luck and fate and love.
I'm thinking we should go back again
to Siena.

# A Piece of Brightness Fell

*Hawaiians and surfers divide the island of Oahu into two:*
*Town, the Waikiki side, and Country, the North Shore of the island.*

One summer, when our daughter Kristy was grown,
John and I rented a place on the North Shore.
Surfing had become his religion,
Sunset, Pipeline, Waimea, his ocean cathedrals.
He prayed for waves just big enough, as summers can be flat.
In Haleiwa, a woman told us about a meteor shower.
It would be beautiful, she said.
We should go to the beach and watch.
So we took a bottle of wine, a towel,
headed out to the little cove I'd found.
We'd just sat on a rock to look up at the sky
where, yes, a piece of brightness fell,
when we felt something buzz in the dark.
Dense and fierce, it didn't seem to want us there.
And we scurried back across the grass.

The next night, though, we returned, to face the invisible,
or to honor whatever was there – we weren't sure which.
Hawaiians say that the side of the island called
*Country* is filled with spirits.
The trade winds clacking in the dried palms
is a lonely, restless sound.
But that night stars streamed down, a sky full of them falling
and we felt safe, took off our clothes,
loved one another in the friendly dark.

It's been seventeen years since John died,
And I have come to understand
the weaving of things.
He's part of the darkness now and speaks to me:
the beautiful eclipse of the moon in March,
the dark bright eye of a sparrow turned my way,
the way the cat let me take the finch she'd caught,
the way it flew up and away when I set it free.

# Memorial

I have erased her name, her face,
though I remember thinking
spitefully, she was not as pretty
as I'd imagined.

Strange, still jealous
even after his ashes, bits of his bones
drifted in June blue waters.
And still, after all these years.

I hadn't ever seen her
but I knew – she was the only one
I didn't know in this circle of friends, family.

My heart twisting into
an animal ball, small and mean,
I said *hello*.
Later, I tore up her check
to the Surfrider Foundation, her card.

The house was crowded, so crowded I couldn't move
from behind the table, laden with gifts of food, flowers,
a fern that still grows.

A tremendous bang from beneath
lifted the floor, let us down.
*Is anyone hurt? Has the baby grand's bad leg given out?*

*Someone go to the living room and see!*
My neighbor Tim knew better.
It was the furnace, a leak;
he ran for the wrench, turned off the gas.

Ric, our Hawaiian friend, a kahuna,
had told me to look for a sign.
I decided it wasn't the paired seagulls
at the ceremony Ric led
at Año Nuevo, where John loved to surf
nor the clouds I tried hard to make a message of.

Later, I could smile.
John knew I was jealous,
inept with wrenches.
*Ka-boom I'm here with you.*
I remember now:

her name was Melanie.

# A Friend Asks Me to Choose One Word

If I could own a word,
just one?
*It would be sky*,
I said to my friend, thinking: then this breeze
making leaf shadows would be mine,
and the way the afternoon light has a soft weft,
a hand like fine silk.

I could claim the sun itself,
the bird calls lacing the air,
bee buzz over clover,
lazy rustle of green.

And this particular sky,
intensely blue
over summer-gold folding
hills, like lions sleeping
under scattered canopies of oak.

But I could never own
all the sky's layered blacks
in the studded night.

# Dream Horse

*after the sculptures of Deborah Butterfield*

In my dream the life-size metal sculpture,
 a horse, not solid, but with open spaces,

the connecting curved plates creating
an abstract of the beautiful animal,

the long nose open from crest to muzzle,
belly barrel open too. And yet he

(I knew it was a he, a bay) looked full
of spirit, ready to come to life.

It came to me how we are all
only partially formed and always

in the process of formation,
partially exposed, partially protected.

In children we can see that easily
as they come into being, opening

and closing and opening again.
I'm thinking now about the passage

from the book my husband read to me
last night, just before I slept:

how Jefferson, so long the optimist
concerning the human spirit,

fell into a depression at his life's end.
And his old friend Adams,

opened into hope at the end of his,
both dying, five hours apart, on July 4.

I'm thinking of the woman on the radio,
called in to quell the rioting kids in the juvenile hall.

They suddenly quieted in their cells
as she whispered, though all could hear,

to the one she knew best on the block,
*Jimmy, What's this about?*

When she told the boys stories of the Japanese prison camp
where she'd been held as a child, they listened too

because she opened herself to them.
I'm thinking of my mother,

who became a waitress, then a wife,
then a woman who wanted to die,

and tried, so she was sent to *Napa State Hospital,*
which she hated. She saw it as *the insane asylum.*

But then she changed again,
and when she was back home,

baked Christmas cookies,
brought them to the others there,

and was happy
for a while.

I want to ride that horse that's open and closed,
broken and whole, keep him close to me

so I can remember that always,
even far along the road,

we can learn to be open.
And that sometimes

it is possible
to make our own miracles.

# Part III
# Sky Holding Fall

# You

## I

You, Mother, with a face of sky and of dirty snow,
you who gaze back at me from the mirror
when I'm feeling low.
You, silent and shut and feeling sorry for everyone
until some wheel inside turns and it's a gift for no reason,
a party for Renie's 80th and will I dance for her?

## II

Sometimes it seems I can call to tell you
how you'd like Alan, how he cooks for me,
how your granddaughter is to be married on the beach.
How maybe on this day between rains
I'll drive up the coast to see you
through gouache of green fields, black tracery of winter oaks –
is gouache the right word?
It is, and there is Van Gogh's *Corridor in the Asylum*,
so like the hospital in Napa
where you were sent,
and cured for a while,
its rings of arches filled with light.

## Synthesis

The room went white,
the doctor's words a buzzing of wasps,
and God was nowhere in the loud no color.

Then Alan held on to me,
pulled me out of the cotton batting of morphine,
where God also did not exist.

And still the electric current between us,
in the bed he made with his own hands
of Port Orford Cedar, his hand cupping

the breast with the crescent scar,
moving down my belly, concentric rings of light
moving out until there was nowhere

his body ended and mine began,
and God was there in the fire.
And still, we sleep in the bed,

make love in the cedar bed,
the wood darker now, but the bed still the boat
where we set out into night together,

leaving day behind,
turning and turning
under the miraculous stars.

# That Instable Object of Desire

*In the oldest dreams of old men, women's breasts still remain…*
*medals, emblems of their love.*   Duane Michals, photographer

rooms full of breasts
rooms darkened to protect the photographs

a young woman holding her shirt up
with her teeth,
on her head a rhinestone diadem
old breasts, empty, pendulous
cactus bud breasts,
pears as breasts
figs, lemons, persimmons,
breasts over Yosemite Falls

the Arbus waitress at a nudist camp,
hers pert and tanned, her order book
tucked into her apron pocket

I'm remembering nursing Kristy –
that night coming home in the car,
the perfect arc of the Sonoma moon in the sky

I'm thinking of tipis, yurts, hogans, kivas
of California tule houses,
of duomos and geodesic domes

I'm thinking of the crescent scar
on my now slightly smaller right breast,
of the clinical words:
lumpectomy, mastectomy,
of Rachael Carson whose breasts were burned
with an x-ray machine, the treatment that didn't save her life,
of how that little scar saved mine
and how lucky that was

I'm thinking of all the women who get treatment
too late
or not at all

for a while, in that dimly lit gallery in Florence,
I wandered in the world of the breast –
*That Instable Object of Desire*

## Fallen Leaf Lake

I make coffee, put biscuits in a sack,
crackers for the minnow trap
while Alan goes to get the tackle box, the poles,
the lake, smooth floating silver spoons of light.

We climb down the hillside to the dock,
step into the borrowed aluminum boat
and head out, a knife
cutting morning silence.

Toward Cathedral Peak,
gleaming necks like feathered arrows,
sleek green Mergansers slice into water for prey.
Alan casts the other way.

But from afar
one duck catches the glitter of the wriggling bait.
And in a flash
is caught on the hook.

He reels the bird in, carefully
pulls the flapping struggling wild thing
into the boat, cradling it in one arm and
reaches needle-nosed pliers down the long throat.

I hold my breath.
*Can't pull the hook out without doing more damage –*
his voice full of gravel or tears.

He cuts the line as close to the hook as he can
and releases the terrified creature

which dives, then rises up
and flies toward Mt. Tallac,
the quiet of the morning
in his wake.

# Lowpensky Lumber

A country song echoes through the warehouse,
cedar and summer dust.
The words unintelligible, but the tempo nostalgia,
melody in the minor key of longing.

At seventeen, I rode with a boy out Refinery Road to Avon,
past the slough, the railroad tracks
or the road through Franklin Canyon,
low-slung oaks tracing desire's deliberate turns,
a September sky holding fall.

Now I sit in this red truck, waiting;
you in the dark loft
draw out the best pieces of Alaskan yellow,
and the slide of wood on wood sings too.

We stack the eight quarter-planks
on the rack in rhythm,
and climb in.
I'm old enough to have learned
how things can change in a beat.
In the truck you open the window
to the tune's fading drift
and I slide close.

## Meditation on Darkness

Farmers carry lanterns to cows
sleepy in barns before dawn.
Ambient light makes stars and planets disappear,
though they are still traveling the old sky roads,
carrying their rocks –
some with circling moons over their shoulders.

Dark is beautiful and dangerous.
It is not in baryonic clouds.
It is not antimatter.
But dark energy, dark matter are nearly everything.
And all that we can touch or see,
all we think we know,
only a tiny fraction of the universe.
The rest, mystery.

Is darkness those instincts we label animal,
inexplicable eruptions of human cruelty:
Lord of the Flies, Beelzebub,
the perverse desire in those three bored boys
who wanted to see someone die?
Or the Jim Jones order to kill the children, babies first?

What I really wanted to write about was
the beauty of dark far from the city
full of swimming stars, shimmering crickets,
and sleep, that other form of dark that matters,
how it heals us,
makes us think in metaphors,
lights up the paths in our heads,
and helps us find the way,
or lose it for a while.

# Lanny Lane, Squaw Valley

*for Susan Perkins 1943 -1979*

One filigreed wing bent up at an angle,
the rest of it smashed on the asphalt.

Susan died on a bend in the road
when a logging truck smashed into her.

I bent to pick it up;
the wing broke from the butterfly's body.

I know she would have taken it up more carefully.
All those years ago, we planned to grow old together.

The way she would have painted it, each scalloped black stripe,
the creamy gold of it, the narrow ragged edge where I broke it.

I went back to the bend in Lanny Lane where I found it:
the rest was gone, blown away or picked up by someone like me.

Susan was driving; the trucker came around the bend,
        curved out of his lane.
She swerved, saved Arnold and their son Miles, ten,
        sitting between them.

Now, holding the wing up to the window, how the light shines through
the lacy veins where the scales have been scraped off.

Then, how Arnold's piercing, bending cry from their bedroom,
smashed into me when he came home to the house so full, so empty.

The way, when I lifted it from the dresser to look at the
        arch of the wing,
it floated off – as if it wanted to fly.

# Night Flight

Closing in around the boat
the darkness swarms
like bumblebees.
The water, impossibly turquoise blue that day
now syrupy black, glittering.
Shadows of houses, towers, trees
waver, black on black.
The crescent moon, fragile,
shivers in the canal.

We two, nearly undone
by Venice, hurtle
toward the end of the dream.

## Salmon Creek Beach

An armada of high clouds sails down the coast.
Below that a line of fog, a ghost train.
From far out, great waves rumble toward the shore.

Young men wade out too far;
children play at the shoreline as if no one had ever told them,
*Never turn your back to the sea.*

At Salmon Creek last year, a woman walked her dog at evening
as she often did. The morning waves returned their swollen bodies,
kept their souls.

John liked to surf here at Salmon Creek,
always went out on New Year's, no matter how cold.
The waves are wild today; no one is out.

Everything looks the same but keeps changing,
beautiful and ancient: the small boats heading out;
the fishermen with long arched poles.

In Bodega, by the narrow, white-spired church,
the single grave: a cross, a teapot filled with flowers
for Elizabeth, 32 years, 9 months and 4 days old in 1862.

In the store across the road, the antique bottles,
the crystal wine glasses etched with roses. Somehow, they survived
all the rolling uncertainty, all the sad lovely tumult.

# Part IV
# Boat Full of Sky

# Mockingbird in an Apple Tree at a Gathering of Poets in Petaluma

The mockingbird gives us his full
late-morning repertoire.
He seems to know his audience:
whistles, chortles, whips out
quick triplets, then slides
into plaintive calls,
a master of form and style, heart breaking
into the summer sky.

If only the words would come to me,
from my own soul and seem, like his songs,
so effortless and unrehearsed.
But I know he shows up for work
every single day, trying out a new tune,
practicing each of the old.

It's not as if he has an easy life.
The mockingbirds on my street
are gone, all. The adaptable crows,
with their feathers of metal,
their bossy caws, have taken over.

This bird has such sweet songs to sing:
on the abundance of bugs in the orchard,
on the ripening striped Gravensteins in the trees,
perhaps on the sweetness of his love.
And for every miraculous solo,
the poets and the grasses
clap softly.

# It Is Possible

*"Death's Head Moth," Van Gogh 1899*

It is possible that things will not get better,
that the current journey into darkness –
men in black masks bearing black flags –
will not stop, but continue to wind on its twisted
and muddy and bloody way.
It is possible that calla lilies are not symbols of resurrection
but of death.
The death's head moth with four bright animal eyes
on its scalloped dusty wings sees nothing.
It is possible that the intricate pattern
etched across the beautiful span
means nothing.

Except that we are all of us
headed in the same direction.
It is possible that the earth's plates
will shift once more beneath the sea,
that waters will roil and race
to take back the land again,
possible that I will not wake beside you,
or that you or I will give in to the old terror.

And yet the green oak trees
still hug the long-parched hills,
and the apple was not the end of all good.

# Yes

I did it.
I went with him
and it changed my life.
But then my life
had already been changed.

You died.
I was still alive.
You had said you didn't want me
to be alone.
That was kind.

He invited me,
and I went.
So soon, though,
maybe too soon –
only three months, a little less,
to tell the truth.

He told me about the roses
growing on the fences
along the vineyards,
red for Alicante and Beaujolais,
white for champenoise and chardonnay.

We flew over the quilted land,
over the oak trees
that I've loved forever,
up with the red-tailed hawks, the ravens,
up with all the beautiful raptors
and I thought of kissing him.

And if I could go back
to that place now,
I would,
and kiss him this time.

But still, I would think of you,
I would.

# Why I Still Have Hope

The last story on the NPR news yesterday:
*So three men go into a bar.*
*No, it's not a set-up for a joke.*
*They entered with guns to rob the place.*
*But let me tell you first, no one was hurt.*
Later, videotapes revealed a couple
sitting in a booth,
completely caught up in a kiss
the whole time, oblivious of the men,
who left with a bag full of money.

The way the grocery store parking lot attendant
gestured me to a space with an elegant sweep of his arm
then pulled it into his chest, bowing low to the ground.

How the steep hills along Interstate 5,
lately long parched,
are now finally lush with April grass,
spilling swaths of poppies,
mustard and blue lupin.

And perhaps most hopeful of all:
the Cloud Appreciation Society,
recently formed,
has thousands of members,
more every day.

## Sappho's Fragments

for all the violet tiaras,
all the woodlots blooming in spring
for all the finches singing their hearts out
all the cats yowling in heat
     and the swans who have lost their mates
for all the hawks spiraling down
        in the clutches of love and destiny
for all the threads undone
the latches unfastened
the hinges rusted and broken
     the rings cast into the sea
for all the letters gone unanswered
     by lovers who have left
for all those shackled by love
and those lonely in their beds
the only balm:
the balm of sadness in song

# Covid Days

Last night, in my dream, crystal wine glasses,
showers of them, spilling down,
shattering soundlessly
into a bottomless well.

In our bed, I woke again,
to the buzzing, anxious dark.
Maybe it's just these days, the heavy fog
of helplessness weighing us down.

Or the memory of last night,
my husband filling the kitchen with angry arrows,
all aimed at me, I thought.
Maybe part of the dark flurry
were darts of my own stifled anger, at him.

Maybe some of the barbs were remnants of fury
at the man with the strange pompadour
and his endless *fantastic* in the midst of a crisis
he can't seem to see.

And now this morning, gloomy still,
and still last night's anger
hanging in the silence as we drink coffee.
Then it condenses as words,
dripping bitterly
from both of us.
Then silence again.

But he takes my hug, at first stiffly,
then returns it, gives in a little,
letting one arm linger around my shoulders
and goes out.

Soon, the hammer's *crack crack crack*
as he works on the new back stairs
and the sharp clean smell of the cedar shingles
reminds me of what I should have said
instead. Now *I* feel like the mean one.

Last week the back door opened
to a three-foot drop, dirt clods
and piles of lumber.
He just kept going out to work,
knowing exactly what tool,
screw or nail to use:
maybe a marlin spike,
maybe a drift, knowing
exactly what's level
and plumb
and what's not.

I envy him, wish I had his steady way.
I hesitate, procrastinate,
and when I finally face it and try,
I can't make up my mind.
Which thing is both like and unlike?
Which word has the right tension, right sound?
How many thousands of times
have I clicked on *tools/thesaurus*?
How many hours spent online
looking for a bird, for *abracadabra*,
for the names of clouds, dark matter,
of our current scourge?

Too often, I've given up, put it on the back burner,
stored everything in the Dropbox
where poetry lives
and poems die from neglect.

But as the power saw whirls and whines its high-pitched song,
I think maybe I'll try hammering away
at what's impossible to say.
Maybe I'll drop some wine glasses
down the well, listen for the shatter
and the echo. Maybe I'll plumb
my awkward wobbles, my anger.
After all, it's Semicolon Day;
why not connect?

*Only connect!* Forster says
The glass breaking in my dream:
the glassy walls of the Marabar Caves.
Why do we humans find it so hard?
Carpenters: joiners who connect wood to wood.

What they call horses
support the farmed mahogany treads and risers.
I open the door he made with ten lights,
with its brass cast-relief knob,
step out, walk down, and cross the tumbled bluestone
to the pond he created
where he sits on its lip
in the sun.

## Boat Full of Sky

Was she thinking of her husband in Paris?
Of the young woman both loved
dead of tuberculosis?
Of her translation of *The Tale of Genji*,
all the copies of the manuscript burned
the day before publication
in the aftermath of the great Tokyo earthquake of 1923?

Akiko describes a worn-out boat
abandoned on a beach,
filled with water reflecting the sky.

From this emptiness, she began again.

# Morning

It waits now, before birdsong,
a patient stillness.

It waits
for a sky full of music
as it was in the old dawns here,
waits for paired Monarchs,
trios, a winged kaleidoscope.

Waits for itself as it was
before DDT,
before Monsanto and monocrops,
before the plundered forests.

As after fire, green returns,
morning light holds possibility.

And that one Anise Swallowtail
my husband photographed
and framed,
yesterday's gift out of the blue,
says perhaps
it is not yet
too late.

# Begin

*Hawaiian Ti leaves are used in spiritual ceremonies, for leis and traditional hula skirts, and to wrap food.*

Begin with persimmon leaves, green
oars pushing through a deep blue sky.
Or begin with schooling fish

glittering in a high lake.
No – always begin with song
tumbling from invisible birds.

Begin with now and the way those two
Chinese Elm branches reach
for each other and the sky.

Begin with an offering of Ti leaves.
Begin with a saltwater cleansing.
Walk into the waves.

Begin with a piece of fruit,
a perfect peach, or a fat blackberry.
Begin with a baby's first cry. Begin

with reaching out
of your loneliness
to another's.

# We Could Have Died, but for Small Miracles

I remember that stone in the stream.
I like to go back to that everyday miracle
which appeared just at my feet. And by everyday
I mean there was no flash of radiance;
the mountain did not speak to me.

But there it was: an ordinary stone, like a large gray egg.
Hawaiians use them for cooking a pig in a pit as well as for prayer.
And I like to remember the cliffs from which the stone must have come,
the steep Hawaiian *pali* with their tangles of green,
to remember how the sweat ran down my face and between my breasts,
as I ran by the waves rolling in,
like even to recall the dogs barking and snarling at me.

And by the stone, I mean *hina* stone, a woman's prayer stone.
And by the dogs I mean adrenalin, how it lets you know you're alive.
And by miracle I mean how our friend Ric,
who could recite the names of all his Hawaiian ancestors,
knew the old ways, told us later
how to treat the stone kindly, giving it *ti* leaves, sea water.

And I mean hope
when there was no cure for the cancer John had.
Even though he's gone,
when I go back to that stream trailing down to the beach,
back to the stone he and I brought home,
I remember
hope.

And I mean that trip when I returned the hina to North Shore –
that summer when John died –
and dropped it into the deep

from a ragged borrowed boogie board at Sunset Beach
where John liked to surf – I was farther out than I'd ever been –

saw it leave my hand, go down,
right where the line-up would be
when the waves were big in the fall.

And the miracle is
that for a moment at least, when I remember again,
he's still here.

And I *did* see that rainbow; Ric saw it too,
lying like a silk scarf on the sea below the Seven Sacred Pools
where John and our daughter and I had hiked when he was well.

And the miracle is, forty years later –
after the death of John, who surely couldn't die,
so strong, so brown, so wedded with the waves,
in spite of that small hard spot in my breast
discovered the next year, quite by accident –
I'm still here,
and what I mean by miracle is
this warm bright August morning.

# Message

You're on that side;
I'm on this.
And here I am with another.
Once, I called him by your name.

Sometimes in dreams
when you're coming home
I don't know what to do with his being here.
In the dreams, houses by water, and
wings, and boats that are beds.

You rode waves as if you had wings.
Now he makes houses into sailing ships:
the kitchen a galley with high shelving,
what used to be our bedroom
now a pilot house.
I write and look out
at the same trees you saw
in skies which still fold spring into fall.
This is our home:
yours, mine;
now mine, his.

The first time I said *love* to him
after the glider ride and my undeniable
greed for his kiss,
he said *I don't know what love is.*

Einstein said that gravity cannot be held responsible
for people falling
in love.
I chose to jump.

# The Moon and the Room and the Windowsill

that September night as we lay sleepless,
the moon spilled into the room,
soaking the rumpled clothes on the floor

so that hard words spoken
melted as we did, into one another

and the moon and the room
and the windowsill
and us there, still breathing

# Breath

We were beginning to stir after savasana
the corpse pose, in which one lies supine:
wings of the nose, root of the tongue,
spine and forehead and limbs all soft and easy,
stray thoughts just clouds passing through.

Though sometimes mine are more like bumper-cars,
this time, for an instant,
I was breathing with the universe,
stars floating out
and rolling back in like the tides,
the darkness of space lightening, then deepening,
galaxies sailing gracefully
toward the edge of nothing,
then returning once more to the center.

When I got home I asked my husband,
from the kitchen where I chopped onions and celery,
*Do you know if they've decided*
*whether the universe is expanding or contracting?*
He called out, *There've been budget cuts.*
*It's shrinking.*

And then I heard a woman on the radio
who said we take in with each breath
some of the dust of the Gobi Desert,
the Sahara, the Serengeti Plains.
She said that we breathe in the dust of stars
and then, of course, we breathe it out again.

The earth is ever decomposing,
releasing the dust of graves.

We inhale particles of pharaohs and emperors,
motes of slaves and concubines,
of Black Elk on his eagle bier.

Today at coffee,
I asked a friend what she thought.
She pointed out *We don't seem to breathe in
wisdom with the dust.*
She says the universe has been expanding
ever since the Big Bang.
Which would explain why the gaps are widening
between nations and tribes and factions and sects,
why the divorce rate is high,
why families feud,
why so many appear to be eager
to gallop toward Apocalypse.

Still, if I lie down in my little death,
and close my eyes,
and take a deep, slow breath,
I can see the Milky Way.

# Acknowledgements

Surfboards (as "The Quiver"), *Willard and Maple*, 2008

Ode to Broken Things, *Willard and Maple*, 2008; *Digital Paper*, 2009

Gliding, *I-70 Review*, 2013

Message, *Willard and Maple*, 2008; *Flyway*, 2009; *The Widows' Handbook, Kent State U.*, 2015

Synthesis, *Grasslimb*, 2009

Fallen Leaf Lake, *Louisville Review*, 2010

Some Birds, *Old Red Kimono*, 2010; *Sierra Nevada Review*, 2010; *Turning a Train of Thought Upside Down*, Scarlet Tanager Press, 2012; *poetrymagazine.com*, 2015

April: Irene, *Many Mountains Moving*, 2009

Red-Tailed Hawk, *Cadillac Cicatrix*, 2008

She Sewed, (as Wheeler-Wilson, 1900-1920) *Willard and Maple*, 2008

The Blue and the Dark, *Marin Poetry Center Anthology*, 2017

Sunday, *Squaw Valley Review*, 2009; *Front Range Review*, 2010

A Piece of Brightness Fell, *Flyway*, 2009

Lowpensky Lumber, *Stringtown*, 2011

Meditation on Darkness, *Dos Passos Review*, 2013

Salmon Creek Beach, *I-70 Review*, 2013

Yes, *Blue Lake Review*, 2012

Sappho's Fragments, *poetrymagazine.com*, 2015; *Ship of Fools*, 2010

The Moon and the Room and the Windowsill, *Soundings East*, 2009; *Willow Review*, 2010

Boat Full of Sky, *Dos Passos Review*, 2014

Morning, *California Fire & Water: A Climate Crisis Anthology*, 2020

Covid Days, *When Covid Came to Visit, ed Thelma Reyna,* (as "Semper Virens") 2021

Dream Horse, *Sisyphus*, Summer, 2020

That Instable Object of Desire, *Levure Litteraire*, Issue 8

Lanny Lane, Squaw Valley, (as For Susan Perkins) *Stickman Review, 2009*

Breath, *Slant*, 2007; *Red Wheelbarrow*, 2008

## About the Author

**Judy Bebelaar** has a fat folder labeled with a red heart. It is full of notes – heartfelt, sweet and sometimes funny – from her students in San Francisco public high schools where she taught for 37 years. She and her students won many writing awards, both local and national. Her prize-winning poetry has been published widely in magazines and anthologies including *The Widows' Handbook, River of Earth and Sky*, and *the Squaw Valley Review. Sky Holding Fall* began as a chapbook called *Walking Across the Pacific*. Her non-fiction book, *And Then They Were Gone: Teenagers of Peoples Temple from High School to Jonestown* (co-authored with Ron Cabral), has won ten awards and honors.